Where Is
Mount Rushmore?

by True Kelley

illustrated by John Hinderliter

Penguin Workshop
An Imprint of Penguin Random House

For Steve, again—TK

PENGUIN WORKSHOP
Penguin Young Readers Group
An Imprint of Penguin Random House LLC

Library of Congress Control Number: 2014042867

ISBN 9780448483566   10 9 8 7

Contents

Where Is Mount Rushmore?

In 1924, the world-famous sculptor Gutzon Borglum and his thirteen-year-old son took a trip together out west. They left their home in Connecticut and, days later, got off a train in Rapid City, South Dakota. Only about six thousand people lived in Rapid City. South Dakota had been a state for only thirty-five years. The Borglums felt they were in the middle of nowhere. They actually were smack-dab in the center of the United States.

Gutzon had come to South Dakota to see if he could find a mountain to carve into the biggest sculpture in the country. He was a patriotic man, and his idea was to give America a sculpture to glorify its greatness. Perhaps it could be huge carvings of great Americans with heads as high as the tallest buildings. What an amazing idea! But many people thought it was crazy. And no one, not even Borglum himself, realized how hard it would be to do.

Gutzon and his son, Lincoln, traveled about twenty-five miles southwest of Rapid City to nearby Keystone, a mining town farther into the backwoods. From there, a South Dakota state forester led them on horseback, following logging trails into the wild country of the Black Hills.

The Black Hills is an area 120 miles long and sixty miles wide. It rises up four thousand feet and more. It is like an island in the middle of the treeless prairie. From the rolling grasslands, the dark green ponderosa pine trees on the hills look black. With steep slopes, deep canyons, rocky ledges, and clear streams, it is rugged but very beautiful country. It is home to many animals, like elk, rattlesnakes, bison, prairie dogs, mountain lions, mountain goats, frogs, birds, and fish. There are medicinal and edible plants, wild raspberries, and flowers. It's no wonder the Lakota Sioux called it sacred land.

The Borglum party clambered up steep, craggy slopes to the top of the tallest mountain, Harney Peak. All around was a wonderful view. Far away, Gutzon could see a granite mountain. It stood higher than the surrounding peaks. That would be the place for his giant sculpture!

The name of the mountain was Mount Rushmore.

Today, huge six-story-high carved heads of presidents George Washington, Thomas Jefferson, Theodore Roosevelt, and Abraham Lincoln gaze out from high on the granite face of Mount Rushmore. Borglum overcame an incredible number of obstacles to create this great national monument. He said it was like waging a one-man war. With his combined drive and talent, he was probably the only man of his time who could have succeeded. For many reasons, it would be impossible to do such a project today.

Mount Rushmore is a major tourist attraction for South Dakota. It has become a symbol of patriotism and pride for many Americans. But people from all over the world travel to marvel at it. Even so, there are people who think it should not ever have been made.

CHAPTER 1
The Black Hills

Throughout history the Black Hills, rising dramatically from the Great Plains, have impressed all who've seen them. They are called hills, but they are the highest mountains east of the Rockies . . . and west of the Alps! Harney Peak, at 7,242 feet, is the tallest.

The Black Hills are some of the oldest hills in North America: sixty million years old. French trappers named them *Côtes Noires*; that means Black Sides. The Lakota Sioux called them *Paha Sapa*—the sacred mountains and place of spirits.

How did these hills get plopped in the middle of the plains around them?

More than two billion years ago, there were only layers of sand, clay, and gravel deep beneath an ancient sea. Over many years, they turned into sedimentary—or layered—rock. Heat and pressure changed it into a type of rock called *mica schist*. Then, 1.5 billion years ago, hot liquid rock oozed from below and joined with the mica to make granite. Sediment piled on top of that.

LAKOTA SIOUX

Seventy million years ago, at the time of the dinosaurs, the molten granite rock was still below the surface of the earth. Over thousands of years, the rock cooled and rose up. The Black Hills were born. As the sea dried, wind, ice, and rain wore away the sediment on top of the granite core.

Beautiful stone towers like the Needles emerged.

Gutzon Borglum knew the granite of these hills was great for sculpting. There were pockets of schist material inside the rock that were not so good, however. The schist could cause some trouble for a sculptor. Also embedded in the rock in parts of the Black Hills were precious metals like silver, tin, and gold.

Around the Hills

High, flat prairie land surrounds the Black Hills. Caves formed in the limestone under those prairies. The Wind Cave, now a national park, is one of the longest caves in the world (132 miles have been explored so far). All around that high land is an area of slightly indented reddish sandstone and shale a few miles wide. Dinosaur and mammoth bones are still found in the red dirt. The Sioux called it "the Racetrack." According to their legend, an ancient race occurred there between birds (two legs) and mammals (four legs) to decide if man (two legs) would eat buffalo (four legs) or buffalo would eat man. Outside the Racetrack is a hard sandstone ridge called the Hogback.

At 6,040 feet, Mount Rushmore is taller than the mountains around it. The Lakota Sioux called it "Six Grandfathers." Later, settlers named it Cougar Mountain, Sugarloaf Mountain, Slaughterhouse Mountain, and Keystone Cliffs.

In the end, it came to be named for a New York lawyer, Charles E. Rushmore. How strange! Charles was on business for a tin company in the Black Hills. In 1885 he was staying in a log cabin in the hills. He asked his guide what the mountain was called. The guide answered that he didn't know, so it must be Mount Rushmore! It was a joke! But the name stuck.

Charles E. Rushmore

CHAPTER 2
The Sioux and the Gold Rush

The Lakota Sioux controlled the Black Hills area before it became part of South Dakota. Their most famous chiefs were Crazy Horse and Sitting Bull.

Crazy Horse

Sitting Bull

Paha Sapa, the Black Hills, was a very special place for the Sioux. They didn't live there. But it was where they hunted elk, bison, and deer. They gathered berries, plants, and medicines there. More than a source of earth's gifts, it was a sacred place where the spirits of dead warriors lived. Young braves went alone on "vision quests" in Paha Sapa, seeking wisdom from the Great Spirit.

The Sioux believed that land and sky couldn't be owned. However, by the 1850s, the United States was pressing in on their sacred lands. The Sioux did not welcome the intruders. The US

Army built forts and stationed soldiers in them. They were there to protect trappers, gold-seekers, and settlers heading west. The US Army thought of the Sioux as enemies. US troops attacked their villages and killed women and children.

The Sioux were one of the most powerful tribes in North America. They successfully resisted US soldiers in small battles and skirmishes until a treaty was signed in 1868. The treaty promised the Sioux that white people would not enter their lands without invitation. All of South Dakota and west of the Missouri River, including the Black Hills, would be theirs forever. "Forever" turned out to be only eight years.

Why did the United States break the treaty? Because of gold. There were rumors of gold in the hills. In 1874, General George Custer marched in with a thousand soldiers. Custer claimed that he and his men were only doing a survey of the land. They were really looking for gold. After three

weeks, they did find some—but barely ten cents'
worth! Still, this was enough to start a gold rush.
The headline in a local paper said, "Prepare for
Lively Times!"

At first, US soldiers were ordered to stick to the treaty and keep miners out of Indian territory. But by 1875, they couldn't stop the flood of fifteen thousand miners from ripping up the ground of those sacred hills.

Boomtowns like Deadwood and Keystone sprang up. A huge gold strike was found, and the Homestake Mine opened. It hired many Europeans and people from other parts of the world. Chinese people came to run laundries and restaurants. Years later, the mine would be one of the first big sponsors of the Mount Rushmore monument.

Wild West Characters

The gold rush boomtowns near Mount Rushmore attracted some colorful characters.

Wild Bill Hickok was a famous lawman, a skilled marksman, and a professional gambler. He claimed to have killed thirty-six men in gunfights. He also said he had wrestled a bear and killed it with a knife. He died in Deadwood in 1876, when he was shot during a poker game.

Calamity Jane was an army scout. She and Wild Bill were friends. Like Wild Bill, she was a storyteller and often exaggerated her own adventures. She was tough, but was admired for her kindness. She died in 1903.

The United States tried to buy the land from the Sioux for $6 million. They would not sell. Crazy Horse had said, "One does not sell the earth on which the people walk."

That did not stop the United States. In 1875, President Ulysses S. Grant ordered all Indians to move to small parcels of land called reservations. When the Sioux didn't, the US Army declared war against them.

Despite Sioux victories at Rosebud and Little Bighorn, the Indians were no match for the US Army. By 1877, Crazy Horse had been killed and Sitting Bull had fled to Canada. The Indians surrendered and were forced onto reservations like Pine Ridge, near Mount Rushmore.

Not only were they robbed of their land, but the Indians fell sick with terrible diseases brought by white people—smallpox, measles, and cholera. The Indians were also starving. A railroad built across the plains in the 1860s disrupted the feeding grounds of the buffalo that Native

Americans depended on. Sometimes, passengers on trains shot buffalo for sport and left them to rot. In 1850, there had been thirty to sixty million buffalo. By 1889, there were around six hundred!

The desperate and starving Sioux were forced to sign an agreement in 1876 that promised them food. In return, they gave up seven million acres of land, including the Black Hills.

They were blackmailed into giving up their land. It was a shameful moment in US history. It was on this land that Mount Rushmore, often called the "Shrine of Democracy," would be built.

CHAPTER 3
Gutzon Borglum

Gutzon Borglum was born on March 25, 1867. He was the son of Danish immigrants who had moved to Idaho in 1864. Gutzon was raised in a large family by his stepmother. Even as children, Gutzon and his younger brother, Solon, were very artistic, and both grew up to be famous sculptors.

Auguste Rodin

By the time he was seventeen, Gutzon knew that art would be his life. He went to California to study painting. In 1889, he married one of his teachers, who was twice his age. They traveled to Paris where Gutzon studied under the great sculptor Auguste Rodin. From then on, Gutzon Borglum knew he wanted to be a sculptor. But he wasn't successful in Europe, and his marriage was failing.

Gutzon left his wife and boarded a ship to go back to the United States in 1901. On the ship, he met Mary Montgomery. After divorcing his first wife, he married Mary in 1909. They had two children, Lincoln and Mary.

Gutzon was a very hard worker, and he worked fast. He could have a small sculpture ready to cast in fifteen minutes! His energetic personality carried over into his sculptures. They were full of life and movement. He could be charming, which helped him win jobs for many pieces of public art. Among many others, he did bronze sculptures of President Abraham Lincoln and the Civil War general Philip Sheridan. His head of Lincoln is in the Capitol Rotunda in Washington, DC.

Casting a Sculpture

This method of making a sculpture has many steps. First, a sculpture is formed out of clay and covered with a layer of plaster. The plaster dries and hardens. Then it is cut apart and taken off of the original sculpture. The empty shell of plaster is called a *mold*. Hot liquid metal, such as bronze, is then poured into the mold. The metal cools and hardens, and the plaster is removed to reveal the final metal sculpture.

One thing Borglum was not good at was managing money. Sometimes he spent more making a sculpture than he earned. Still, he was doing well enough that he bought an estate in Connecticut.

In 1915, a group of people from Georgia came to him with an idea for a giant carving on a mountain near Atlanta. They wanted Borglum to portray General Robert E. Lee. Lee had been the top general of the Southern troops in the Civil War. Borglum loved the idea of very big art. He said, "My big mission in life is to get the American people to look at art in a big way." No one had carved on huge surfaces in modern times. Borglum had to invent new ways to work on such a large scale. He found a clever way to project slides of the carving he wanted to do onto the cliff face. He invented sling seats so carvers could hang in front of the cliff. He figured out how to

carve using small charges
of dynamite. Soon after,
the head of Robert E. Lee
began to emerge from
Stone Mountain in
Georgia.

Borglum and the Ku Klux Klan

While working in Georgia, Borglum got mixed up with a very bad group. He joined the Ku Klux Klan. The Klan started in the South after the South lost the Civil War. It is a group of white people who think they are better than everyone else, especially black people. Borglum's views didn't make much sense. He didn't like immigrants, even though he was the son of immigrants. He didn't like Jews, though he had many Jewish friends. When he left Stone Mountain, he ended his membership in the Klan. It had become an embarrassment for him and for his family.

In 1924, with great showmanship, Borglum unveiled the finished head of Robert E. Lee on the side of the mountain. The rest of the sculpture, Lee leading a group of generals on horses, still needed to be completed.

Unfortunately, Borglum wasn't getting along with the Stone Mountain Memorial Association's board of directors. Borglum was never easy to work with. He liked to argue, and he was sure he was always right! He didn't take criticism well. He was an artist, and he resented anyone who tried to tell him what to do. At times, he could act like a spoiled child.

In Georgia, the people who hired him to carve General Lee were getting impatient. The project was taking too long. It was costing too much. They wanted Borglum to make the sculpture smaller to save money. This enraged him. Borglum threw a tantrum!

The group decided to fire Borglum and hire

another sculptor. When Borglum got wind of this, he smashed the big plaster models of Lee in his studio. He pushed the rest of the models off a cliff, crashing them on the rocks below!

The Stone Mountain group put out a warrant for his arrest! They said Borglum had destroyed property that belonged to them. According to Borglum, he and his assistant fled in a car, chased by police officers who were shooting at them! Finally, they got to safety in the next state. Borglum, however, was known to exaggerate, and that was his version. According to his wife, he just quietly left the state before he could be arrested.

At this low point in Gutzon Borglum's life, South Dakota offered him the chance to make an even bigger sculpture. Of course he jumped at the chance!

Stone Mountain Today

When a new sculptor was hired at Stone Mountain, the board of directors told him to chisel off Lee's hat, because Lee would have never worn a hat in the presence of the ladies who would be viewing him! Eventually, all of Borglum's work was blasted off Stone Mountain, and a new sculpture was made that is a tourist attraction today.

CHAPTER 4
Big Plans

A man named Doane Robinson lived in South Dakota. He was the state historian. He wanted to bring pride as well as tourist dollars to the new state of South Dakota. His idea was to glorify the Old West with a huge sculpture in the Black Hills. Many local people, however, were against carving into their Black Hills. Environmentalists today might agree.

Doane Robinson got in touch with Gutzon Borglum because he had heard of his work in Georgia. He must not have heard how that project turned out!

Borglum promised that his carving would be "the greatest thing of its character in the entire world." Borglum wanted more than a monument about the Old West. He wanted a monument for the whole country. He wanted to carve great American presidents like George Washington and Abraham Lincoln.

Borglum was pretty sure Mount Rushmore was the right place for his sculpture. But he needed to get a closer look. He and his son, Lincoln, camped at the base and climbed with others to the top of the mountain. It was a hard climb. To get up one cliff, they nailed together a ladder of pine branches.

Lincoln later described their climb: "At one point we pyramided three men on each other's shoulders so the top man could loop his lariat over a projecting sliver of rock!" At the top, they raised a flag.

The granite face on Rushmore looked good to Borglum. It was four hundred feet high by about five hundred feet long. Much bigger than a football field! He liked how it got the sun most of the day. He liked that the granite was finely textured and seemed to have no deep cracks.

Borglum also liked that Mount Rushmore was in the center of the country and far from big cities. A city newspaper back east said, "Borglum is about to destroy another mountain. Thank God it is in South Dakota and no one will ever see it." Many local people wanted their beautiful wild areas left alone, too, and they protested loudly. On top of that, the angry group from Georgia sent letters to South Dakota saying that Borglum was a thief.

Borglum wasn't bothered by all the critics. He called them "mere horseflies." Borglum picked four presidents to carve. They would represent the first 150 years of American history. George Washington, the father of the country, was an easy choice.

Thomas Jefferson had written the Declaration of Independence. Abraham Lincoln was Borglum's favorite president (his son was named after him); he had freed the slaves and united the country.

Borglum's final choice was Theodore Roosevelt, president from 1901 to 1909. Why did he choose Teddy Roosevelt? Because Borglum identified with him. Their personalities were much alike. They even looked a bit alike. Roosevelt had died only six years earlier, in 1919. Some thought it was too soon to know if Teddy Roosevelt belonged on the mountain. Democrats wanted Woodrow Wilson. But Borglum had his way.

Who Should Be on Mount Rushmore?

There have been many suggestions of people to be added to the mountain over the years: Dwight D. Eisenhower, John F. Kennedy, Susan B. Anthony, Crazy Horse, John Wayne, and Elvis Presley, among others. But Borglum knew that there was only room for four heads.

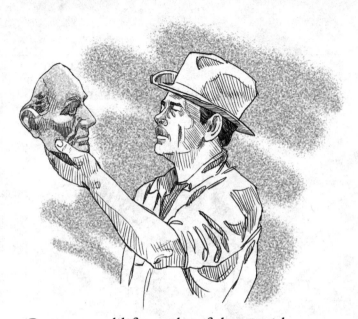

Gutzon used life masks of the presidents to get accurate likenesses of them. Life masks are made by putting liquid plaster or wax on the face of a living person. It is removed after it hardens and then used as a mold to be cast in plaster or other materials.

Gutzon left to go back east for a while. Right away, Doane Robinson started trying to raise money for the project. It proved harder than anyone imagined. Throughout the project, money would always be a problem. Borglum had thought $50,000 would be easy to get from local donations. Instead, the people of South Dakota were only able to give $5,000.

South Dakota senator Peter Norbeck believed in the project from the start. In fact, without him, Mount Rushmore could have never been done. Touring by car was beginning to be popular, and Norbeck worked to build better scenic roads. He imagined a future where cars full of tourists would come to South Dakota to see Borglum's sculpture.

Throughout the years, the project depended on getting federal money. Senator Norbeck was most responsible for getting it, even in hard times.

With or without money, Borglum was itching to get started. In September 1925, Borglum and his assistant, Jesse Tucker, spent days measuring and studying the mountain. They clambered

all over the steep cliffs. They had to do a lot of careful planning. Borglum made plaster models in his studio with one inch to equal one foot on the final sculpture.

There was no real road yet, but three thousand people came to a dedication ceremony at Mount Rushmore on October 1, 1925. A band played, and soldiers fired salutes. Huge flags were raised on top of the mountain. There were speeches by Senator Norbeck, Doane Robinson, and Gutzon Borglum.

Borglum was a very exciting speaker. He promised that the first head would be finished in a year. But a year later, due to lack of funds, it hadn't even been started. Borglum was determined to keep his vision alive. He spoke to the members of Congress in Washington, DC, and traveled around the United States with a small model asking for money . . . without much success.

Meanwhile, Doane Robinson did a little

better. He got donations from the railroads, local businessmen, and from Charles E. Rushmore himself. For the first time, people (other than Borglum) thought the project might actually happen!

CHAPTER 5
How to Carve Big

It would be impossible to carve a huge mountain with puny hammers and chisels. Borglum planned to use jackhammers, drills . . . and dynamite.

Before starting, many systems needed to be set up. Workers built a rough road for carrying equipment and supplies. They built a power plant three miles away with a power line to the compressors at the site. *Compressors* are machines that use electric power to squeeze air into a small space. The air can then be released in quick bursts to run equipment. Tentacles of air lines ran from the compressors to the jackhammers on the cliffside. Workers carried building supplies up a new 760-step stairway to the top. They had to be tough just to climb to work!

A little town sprang up at the bottom of the cliff
with toolsheds, a blacksmith shop, a bunkhouse,
a studio, a dining hall, a kitchen, and compressor
houses. At the top, they built a repair shop, storage
sheds, a storm shelter, an office, a small studio,
and a maze of walkways. Sling chairs were set up.
They dug a well and dammed a stream. "Rush
more!" was their motto.

In 1927, a ceremony to celebrate the start of drilling was held. A South Dakota congressman had invited President Calvin Coolidge to vacation nearby. The president rode over on horseback and gave a speech. Just by showing up, he gave the project a big boost. Instead of a twenty-one-gun salute in his honor, twenty-one stumps were dynamited in the roadway that was to be built.

In the most dramatic moment of the day, Borglum was lowered over the side of the cliff in a sling chair dangling from a thin cable. Then he drilled the first holes on the mountain. The chair looked very scary, and Borglum looked very tiny on the face of Mount Rushmore. The crowd was awestruck.

The Pointing System

Unlike Stone Mountain, Rushmore's face was too lumpy for projecting images from below to show where to carve. Instead, Borglum used a system called *pointing*. At the top of the head to be carved was a flat, circular plate that was marked by degrees. A thirty-foot beam with two plumb lines hanging from the end was mounted on the plate. It matched a much smaller beam and plate in the studio that sat on the head of the studio model. One inch on the studio model was equal to one foot on the mountain. Matching the exact degrees gave an accurate idea of how deep to cut into the rock.

On October 4, 1927, the real carving began. First, a lot of rock was dynamited away. This was done to get to the more solid granite underneath. Hand-run winches lowered workers in harnesses to drill holes for the dynamite using heavy, air-powered jackhammers.

The workers were Keystone locals. Most had been loggers or miners. It took guts to run a jackhammer while hanging by a thin cable high up on the side of a windy cliff. They were tough men. Still, some quit after the first day!

After the holes were drilled, men called *powder monkeys* put dynamite in the holes and set the charges. When everyone was safely off the mountain—at noon or the end of the day—the blasts went off. By the end of the project, 450,000 tons of rock rested at the bottom of the cliff!

As they got closer to the carving surface, smaller charges were used. The men were careful to leave three to six inches of granite for the final carving. At this point, the sculpted head was an egg shape.

The next stage of carving was done on scaffolding that was bolted to the rock, or from cages that hung down from the winch house. Holes were drilled a couple of inches deep and two inches apart. It was called *honeycombing*. It weakened the rock so that it could be pried off with a steel tool or by hand. Now, the features of the face were roughed in. The final stage was less engineering and more pure art. And Borglum was a great artist.

He studied the sculpture from all sides. Shadows and light changed how it looked. He studied it in rain, snow, and fog, and at all hours of the day. He would look through binoculars from miles away and then rush back to make changes of only a few inches. He would be lowered in his sling chair to paint red lines to show what needed to be fixed. A driller might then take days to make a tiny change. He had to be very careful not to take off too much rock. It couldn't be put back on! Finally, a bumping hammer was used to smooth the rock.

But by December 1927, work on Washington's head hadn't gotten very far. Winter temperatures dropped to twenty-two degrees below zero. Work had to shut down. Worse still, money ran out, and work couldn't start again for one and a half years.

CHAPTER 6
The Big Boss

By 1929, Gutzon Borglum had new bosses. The group was appointed by the president. It was called the Mount Rushmore National Memorial Commission. A South Dakota businessman named John Boland was the head of it. Boland insisted on cutting costs. Borglum tended to spend recklessly and hated Boland. For years, they constantly fought with each other. It was Boland, however, who kept the whole project on track. Many years later, Borglum realized that, and the two men actually became friends.

Borglum and his family moved to a huge ranch near Mount Rushmore. Due to his poor money skills, Borglum almost lost the ranch to the bank. Who bailed him out and saved the ranch? John Boland!

During times when money ran out, men had to be laid off or the job would have to be closed down. In fourteen years, it was closed down so many times that only six and a half years were spent actually working. More than 360 people worked on Rushmore over those years. It was amazing that so many of them remained loyal through all the shutdowns. They had become a close group, proud of what they were making. That was one reason why they did such risky work in below-zero temperatures or when it was so hot you couldn't touch the granite.

What kind of boss was Borglum? They called him "the Old Man" or "the Chief." "He ain't no sweet talker," one worker said. His men knew enough to never disagree with him! He would fire people at the drop of a hat. His secretary claimed she was fired seventeen times! One worker who was never fired was Borglum's son, Lincoln, who worked on the project from beginning to end.

The workers understood that Borglum was a great artist. They knew he did all he could to keep them working, even to the point of using his own money. They admired how he fearlessly used the harness to check their work. Best of all, he told them to stop and have coffee and doughnuts at 10:00 a.m. every day. He invented the coffee break!

Safety on the Jobsite

Borglum looked out for the safety of his men. In a very dangerous workplace, in fourteen years there was never a fatal accident! There were accidents, though. One was a lightning strike in 1938 that set off a dynamite charge. It blew the shoes off a worker. Another time, a huge rock was blasted off the mountain, and it rolled down, flattening trees. It stopped just before the blacksmith shop. The worst accident was when the brake broke on a cage that was carrying men. The cage went shooting down the mountain and slammed to a stop. One man had a broken arm and ribs from jumping out before it hit, and the others were pretty banged up.

By the end of 1929, George Washington's head was almost finished. It was sixty feet tall. His nose was twenty-one feet long! Borglum left an extra inch on the nose to counteract erosion so that it would last at least ten thousand years. That's thinking ahead!

On July 4, 1930, Washington's head was dedicated in a splashy ceremony with two thousand people cheering. The tourists were starting to arrive. Four hundred a day!

The plan was to carve Jefferson next, but the Great Depression had settled in. Funding was harder to get than ever. People had more important things to spend money on. "You can't eat art," they said. No work was done until the end of that summer.

Gutzon had to go to Poland to unveil a statue he had done. He hired an old friend, Italian sculptor Hugo Villa, to oversee the carving of Thomas Jefferson at Mount Rushmore. Little did he know what a complete disaster Jefferson would become.

CHAPTER 7
Big Problems

Gutzon Borglum always seemed sure of himself. But he said, "I confess I have never been free from fear and anxiety over the outcome of every phase of the undertaking."

Mount Rushmore showed Borglum what he could and could not do.

Borglum experienced his worst nightmare on Jefferson's head. He had run into carving trouble many times before. To avoid cracks and flaws in the granite, he rearranged the position of the heads nine times during the project. At first, he had planned to sculpt each president to the waist. But when he started Washington's coat, the rock was too soft.

Hugo Villa was in charge of the carving while Gutzon was away. Villa found big cracks in the rock to the right of Washington's head. Jefferson wouldn't fit there! When Borglum got back from Poland he accused Villa of flattening Jefferson's head and cutting too deep. Villa argued there just wasn't enough room in that spot. Borglum fired him. (He rehired him later when he finally admitted Villa was right.)

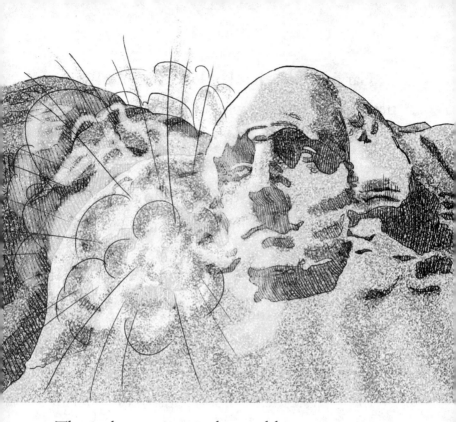

The only answer to the problem was to move Jefferson to the other side of Washington. Borglum had no idea how he would also fit in Lincoln and Roosevelt. But he knew what he had to do.

He blasted Villa's Jefferson off the cliff! Eighteen months of work turned to rubble. John Boland, the man in charge of spending, was furious. What a waste of time and money!

Carving a new head of Jefferson gave Borglum new headaches. It was difficult to find good granite in the new location. After dynamiting ninety feet into the mountain, the workers finally began carving. Then they ran into a big crack in Jefferson's nose. Freezing water in the crack could lop it right off.

"I have no intention of leaving a head on that mountain that in the course of five hundred or five thousand years will be without a nose," Borglum said. He repositioned the head to avoid the crack.

In 1939, six inches of soft feldspar on Jefferson's lip had to be patched with a two-foot square and foot-deep chunk of granite. It's the only major patch on the whole mountain, and it's very hard to see. Jefferson was finished in 1941, and his head is considered the best of all the carvings.

In 1933, the National Park Service took over Rushmore. Harold Ickes, US Secretary of the Interior, was the one in charge of approving money

Harold Ickes

for it. He didn't like Rushmore. He compared it to carving initials on a tree. Even so, he didn't stop the project. Maybe he saw that it was a symbol of hope for Americans during hard times.

By 1936, the National Park Service was really worried that Mount Rushmore might not be finished. They sent an engineer to keep Borglum in line. His name was Julian Spotts.

The Great Depression

October 29, 1929, is known as Black Tuesday. On that day, the US stock market crashed, and many people lost all their money. Banks lost money, too, and many closed. Businesses failed. Some survived by cutting wages and firing people. There were few jobs to be found. People lost their homes and farms.

President Franklin D. Roosevelt started new programs to get jobs back, and to get banks running again. It was called the New Deal. The Great Depression ended when the United States entered World War II in 1941. People and factories were put to work making things for the war.

Spotts made a lot of improvements to the work site. He tried to get Borglum to keep better records and better estimate costs. He also wouldn't let Borglum fire anyone!

It didn't take long for Borglum to blow up. He called Spotts a "brainless jelly bean." Spotts refused to be bullied. They wouldn't speak to each other, and communicated by letter even though their offices were side by side.

Meanwhile, Teddy Roosevelt was placed between Jefferson and Lincoln in an area full of cracks. The workers removed 120 feet of rock. There was only thirty feet left before they would break through to the canyon behind. The ridge of rock connecting to Jefferson was only three feet wide. Borglum must have had nerves of steel! He managed to make Roosevelt fit, but he was far back from the other heads.

Washington, Jefferson, and Lincoln were almost finished. Fifteen thousand tons of granite were blasted away in 1936. Now, the Rushmore project was really rolling.

Franklin D. Roosevelt

CHAPTER 8
Finishing

President Franklin D. Roosevelt dedicated the head of Thomas Jefferson in 1936, during the depths of the Great Depression. Mount Rushmore had come to symbolize the American spirit of getting great things done, even in the worst of times.

Borglum's son, Lincoln, became foreman when he was twenty-two years old. As a boss, he was the opposite of his father. He was calm and easygoing. The men respected him. He was able to work well with Julian Spotts. He wanted things done properly, and was an artist as well.

Borglum and the Lakota Sioux

In 1931, Borglum was horrified when he saw how the Indians lived on the nearby Pine Ridge Reservation. They were starving, and the government wasn't helping them enough. He organized a campaign to get them food, cattle, clothing, and blankets before winter. Borglum later praised the president in 1934 for reforms that helped the Indians.

The Sioux called Borglum "Stone Eagle." They asked him to carve Crazy Horse onto Rushmore. There wasn't room, but he promised to carve a "Great Plains Chief" in Nebraska. Borglum didn't live long enough to see it done. Years later, Korczak Ziolkowski, an old apprentice to Borglum, started carving Crazy Horse a few miles away. Although Korczak died in 1982, the sculpture is still under way.

In September 1937, a huge flag was raised from the face of Abraham Lincoln. A crowd of five thousand people sang "The Star-Spangled Banner."

The head of Lincoln was dedicated. As usual, there were problems. A giant smudge of colored rock ran across Lincoln's left cheek and nose.

Meanwhile, Gutzon Borglum was still at war with the National Park Service. Borglum couldn't stand the government looking over his shoulder. By 1937, the National Park Service had removed itself from the project. Borglum was glad to be done with them—and they were glad to be done with him!

Gutzon chose his own people for a new commission. Once he was getting his own way, things went more smoothly. Now the men could work all year, as long as the temperature was above twenty below zero. In winter, the staging where they worked was wrapped in canvas tarps and heated with coal in barrels. Unfortunately, the tarps trapped the granite dust and smoke. It was terrible to breathe. Years later, some of Gutzon's workers died of lung disease from breathing that granite dust.

Teddy Roosevelt's head was taking shape. Borglum cleverly solved the problem of how

to sculpt Roosevelt's glasses. He made a line to indicate the frame and left most of the frame and lenses to the imagination. It worked!

On the fiftieth anniversary of South Dakota's statehood, twelve thousand people came to the dedication ceremony for Roosevelt's head.

It was held at night with fireworks. Searchlights dramatically lit the presidents. Eighty-three-year-old Doane Robinson, the man who first came up with the idea, was there. Just as he had hoped, South Dakota was proud. And just as Gutzon Borglum had hoped, so was the whole nation.

The Hall of Records

The Hall of Records was to be a cave carved out behind the four heads. An eight-hundred-foot stairway would lead to it. Inside would be statues of great Americans like Benjamin Franklin and Susan B. Anthony, and records of US history. It would explain to people thousands of years in the future what Mount Rushmore was all about.

In 1939, Congress told Lincoln Borglum to stop work on the Hall of Records and finish the faces first, before the money ran out. The Hall of Records was never completely finished.

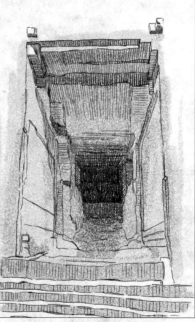

In 1939, Gutzon Borglum was seventy-two years old and in poor health. He had been working on Mount Rushmore for fourteen years. He was again scrapping with the National Park Service. His son, Lincoln, did finishing work on the faces throughout 1940. But Gutzon was still fighting for the project. He traveled to Chicago to make a radio speech promoting Mount Rushmore. On March 6, 1941, Gutzon Borglum, surrounded by his family, died in a Chicago hospital of a heart attack. He was seventy-four.

Gutzon Borglum had believed in Mount Rushmore when others had given up. Keeping the project on track sometimes seemed harder than the actual carving. Without his dream, energy, leadership, and persistence, there would be no Rushmore. No one else could have done it.

Now, Lincoln Borglum was the sculptor as well as foreman. The details on the faces had been finished before his father died. But he spent the summer doing finishing touches: the hair on Jefferson, Roosevelt, and Lincoln; the collars on Jefferson and Lincoln; and Washington's jacket. On October 31, 1941, the drilling stopped, the scaffolds were taken down, and the equipment was put away. The attention of the United States turned to World War II.

Rushmore was declared done.

CHAPTER 9
Mount Rushmore Today

Today, tourists drive past attractions like Reptile Gardens and Bear Country U.S.A. until they get to Mount Rushmore National Memorial.

Popular Tourist Attractions

Mount Rushmore now has more than three million visitors a year! That's about as many as the Statue of Liberty. Yellowstone National Park gets about 3.5 million visitors every year. The Grand Canyon gets five million. Great Smoky Mountains

A model in Legoland

National Park is the busiest one in the United States, with nine million visitors. Walt Disney World is the most visited theme park in the world, with seventeen million visitors every year!

In Denmark, people are proud that Gutzon Borglum was Danish.

Legoland in Billund, Denmark, has a model of Mount Rushmore made out of 1.5 million Lego pieces. Almost two million people a year visit the copy of Mount Rushmore!

On the grounds, the National Park Service finished a huge project in 1991. They built trails, parking, a visitors' center, the historic sculptor's studio, a tepee village, a museum, an amphitheater,

a viewing terrace, and a building with gift shops and restaurants. It cost $40 million. Gutzon Borglum spent less than $1 million in the fourteen years of sculpting the monument!

Visitors from all over the world walk down the Avenue of Flags, approaching the Mount Rushmore viewing terrace. They can look in the studio to see models and tools used in the carving.

They can walk a loop trail to get a closer look at the monument and maybe even see a mountain goat. They can visit the tepee village and learn about the Lakota Sioux.

When people see the heads of the presidents, they are amazed at their size and artistry. The faces are enormous. Each eye is eleven feet wide. The mouths are eighteen feet wide, which is longer than most cars. The Statue of Liberty has a nose that is four and a half feet long. But Washington's nose is twenty-one feet long. One worker said that if it rained, nine men could hide under that nose to stay dry!

Each president is lively-looking and has expression. Washington is stern. Lincoln looks determined. Jefferson seems a little amused.

Roosevelt looks kindly. A lot of this is due to Borglum's clever trick with their eyes. Unlike Greek or Roman statues whose eyes are very blank, Borglum figured out how his faces could have more life. In the middle of each eyeball, he carved a concave bowl that had a two-foot-long rock shaft sticking out of the middle of it. With the play of light and shadow, the eyes look real!

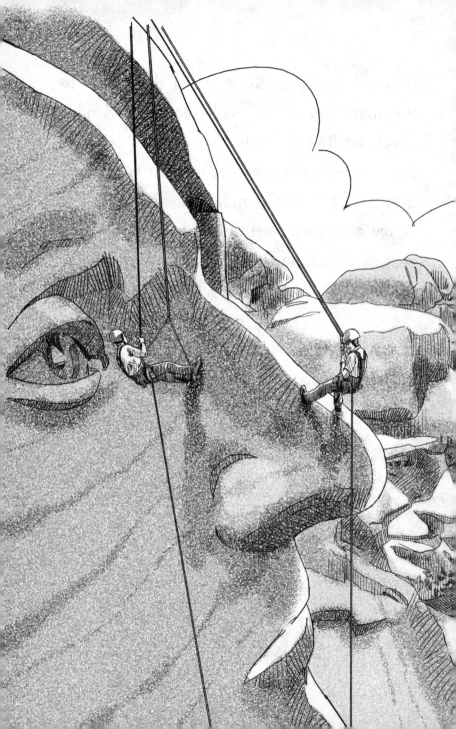

Every year, the National Park Service inspects the carvings for cracks that ice can widen in the winter. Borglum used a mix of granite dust, white lead, and linseed oil to fix cracks, but now a silicon-based material is used. There are three cracks that are watched very closely. One is across Lincoln's nose, one is on top of Washington's head, and one is on the hair on Roosevelt's forehead.

The Sioux and Rushmore

American Indians have reasons to dislike Mount Rushmore. Many think the tourists are intruders on Paha Sapa, their sacred lands. The sculpture itself is built on land stolen from them. In 1971, the American Indian Movement occupied Mount Rushmore in protest. They demanded the return of the land promised to them in the Treaty of 1868.

In 1980, through the Supreme Court, the Sioux won a huge settlement of $102 million. Despite poverty on the reservation, they refused the money! They said the Black Hills had never been for sale. It seems the return of some of the land may be possible someday.

In 2004, a Native American, Gerard Baker, was appointed superintendent at Mount Rushmore. He added new programs and exhibits that now tell the story of the Lakota Sioux and Paha Sapa.

After the 9/11 terrorist attacks, the National Park Service thought that people would be afraid to go to national monuments. But record numbers of

visitors came to Mount Rushmore. Like the Statue of Liberty, Rushmore is a symbol of democracy. Often, people are very emotional when they see it.

Some people still have mixed feelings about Mount Rushmore. One thing is for sure: Rushmore is an amazing feat of engineering. But is it great art or not? Is it a symbol of US pride or self-importance? Is it a national treasure or a national disgrace? Does it add to or ruin the natural beauty of the Black Hills? Every person will react to Mount Rushmore in a different way. The best way to find out how you feel about it is to go see Mount Rushmore for yourself.

Timeline of Mount Rushmore

1820s	Lakota Sioux control the lands of the Black Hills
1823	First white trappers travel through the Black Hills
1868	Fort Laramie Treaty is signed, benefitting the Sioux
1874	General Custer finds gold in the Black Hills . . . gold rush!
1875	President Grant orders Sioux onto reservations
1876	The Battle of Little Bighorn; a treaty forces the Sioux to give up their lands
1877	Crazy Horse is killed and Sitting Bull escapes to Canada
1884–85	Charles E. Rushmore visits the Black Hills
1889	South Dakota becomes a state
1923	Doane Robinson has a monumental idea
1924	Gutzon Borglum and his son, Lincoln, visit the Black Hills
1925	Borglum and his assistant start planning to carve Rushmore
Oct 1925	Rushmore dedication ceremony
1927	President Coolidge attends first marks made on Rushmore
Oct 1927	Carving begins
Jul 1930	The head of Washington is dedicated
1933	The National Park Service takes over Rushmore
1936	The head of Jefferson is dedicated
1937	The head of Lincoln is dedicated
1939	The head of Teddy Roosevelt is dedicated; work stops on the Hall of Records
Mar 1941	Gutzon Borglum dies
Oct 1941	Mount Rushmore is declared finished
1971	The American Indian Movement protests at Rushmore
1980	The Lakota Sioux win in the Supreme Court
1991	The National Park Service finishes a major restoration of the memorial grounds
2004	First Native American superintendent, Gerard Baker, is appointed
2006	Mount Rushmore is featured on the South Dakota quarter

Timeline of the World

Swedish inventor Alfred Nobel patents his invention of dynamite — **1867**

Susan B. Anthony and Elizabeth Cady Stanton form the National Woman Suffrage Association in the United States — **1869**

John D. Rockefeller's empire controls about 95 percent of US oil refining — **1880**

US Congress creates Yosemite National Park — **1890**

General Robert Baden-Powell starts the Boy Scouts — **1908**

Earth passes through the tail of Halley's Comet — **1910**

The Royal Army Medical Corps is the first to store blood for transfusion — **1917**

President Warren G. Harding installs the first radio in the White House — **1922**

John Logie Baird performs the first demonstration of a working television system — **1925**

Gandhi and Jawaharlal Nehru organize a Declaration of Independence by the people of India, which was still part of the British Empire — **1930**

Jesse Owens wins the 100-meter dash at the Summer Olympics in Nazi-controlled Berlin — **1936**

The German zeppelin *Hindenburg* bursts into flames while landing in Lakehurst, New Jersey — **1937**

Albert Einstein writes President Franklin Roosevelt about developing an atomic bomb using uranium — **1939**

The United States enters World War II after Japanese planes bomb Pearl Harbor — **1941**

The United States hires its first female FBI agents — **1972**

Computer scientist Sir Tim Berners-Lee invents the World Wide Web — **1989**

US president George W. Bush declares war on Iraq — **2003**

World population is calculated at 6.5 billion people — **2006**

Bibliography

*Books for young readers

*Falk, Laine. *What Is Mount Rushmore?*. Danbury, CT: Children's Press, 2009.

*Jango-Cohen, Judith. *Mount Rushmore*. Minneapolis: Lerner, 2004.

*Kenney, Karen Latchana. *Mount Rushmore*. Edina, MN: Magic Wagon, 2011.

Larner, Jesse. *Mount Rushmore: An Icon Reconsidered*. New York: Nation Books, 2002.

Ostler, Jeffrey. *The Lakotas and the Black Hills: The Struggle for Sacred Ground*. New York: Viking, 2010.

Smith, Rex Alan. *The Carving of Mount Rushmore*. New York: Abbeville Press, 1985.

*St. George, Judith. *The Mount Rushmore Story*. New York: G.P. Putnam's Sons, 1985.

Taliaferro, John. *Great White Fathers: The True Story of Gutzon Borglum and His Obsessive Quest to Create the Mt. Rushmore National Monument*. New York: Public Affairs, 2002.

White, Mel. *Complete National Parks of the United States*. Washington, DC: National Geographic, 2009.

Websites

www.nps.gov/moru/index.htm

www.pbs.org/wgbh/americanexperience/films/rushmore

www.history.com/topics/mount-rushmore

www.mtrushmore.net

www.bensguide.gpo.gov/3-5/symbols/mountrushmore.html

www.smithsonianmag.com/travel/da_rushmore.html?c=y&page=1

The official South
Dakota State Quarter

The Avenue of Flags at Mo

© Thinkstock, photographed by franciscodiazpagador

US postage stamps from 1974 and 1952 featuring Mount Rushmore

Below: Portraits and signatures of the four US presidents whose faces are on Mount Rushmore

unt Rushmore

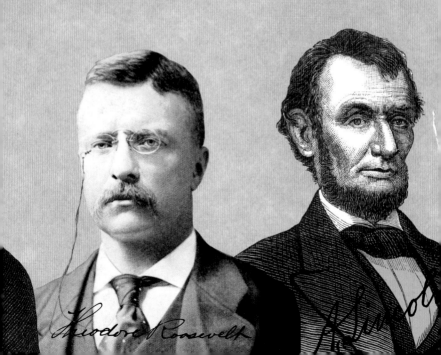